Yiddish Wisdom

Yiddishe Chochma

Illustrated by

Kristina Swarner

CHRONICLE BOOKS

SAN FRANCISCO

For my grandmother, Eva *Chava* Golden.
I love you, Gram. —K.B.S.

Special thanks to Moshe Barlev for his help.

Printed in Hong Kong.

Library of Congress Cataloging-in-Publication Data:
Yiddish Wisdom = Yiddishe Cochma / illustrations by Kristina Swarner
        p.   cm.
    In English and Yiddish (roman)
    ISBN 0-8118-1202-2
    1. Proverbs, Yiddish. 2. Proverbs, Yiddish—Translations into
    English.
I. Swarner, Kristina   95-41292
PN6519.J5Y48   1996   CIP

Book and cover design: Anne Shannon
Cover illustration: Kristina Swarner

Distributed in Canada by
Raincoast Books
8680 Cambie Street
Vancouver, B.C. V6P 6M9

10 9 8 7 6 5 4 3 2 1

Chronicle Books
275 Fifth Street
San Francisco, CA 94103

Yiddish Wisdom

✣

A fault-finder complains even that
the bride is too pretty.

A chissoren, di kalleh iz tsu shain.

A little charm and you are not
ordinary.

A bisseleh chain iz shoin nit gemain.

⁂

An ugly patch is nicer
than a pretty hole.

A mi'ese late iz shener vi a shaineh loch.

⁂

From your mouth into God's ears!

Fun dein moil in Got's oi'eren arein!

A big oven—a small loaf!

A groiser oiven—a kleine challeh!

Nerve succeeds!

Chutspeh gilt!

⚜

One always thinks that others
are happy.

Ainem dacht zich az bei yenem lacht zich.

⚜

No answer is also an answer.

Nit kain entfer iz oich an entfer.

Quiet streams tear away the shores.

Di shtileh vasserlech reissen ein di breges.

⌇

The face tells the secret.

Der ponim zogt ois dem sod.

⌇

The tongue is the pen of the heart.

Di tsung iz der feder fun hartz.

Jack of all trades, master of none.

Fil meloches, vainik broches.

⚮

You can't ride in all directions
at one time.

Me ken nit foren oif alleh yariden oif ain mol.

⚮

Everything revolves around bread
and death.

Alts drait zich arum broit un toit.

When the heart is full, the eyes overflow.

Az dos hartz iz ful, gai'en di oigen iber.

A fool falls on his back and bruises
his nose.

A shlimazel falt oifen ruken un tseklapt zich di noz.

❧

Better the devil you know than
the devil you don't.

Besser mitn taivel vos m'ken eider mitn taivel

vos m'ken im nit.

If you're going to do something wrong,
enjoy it!

Az me est chazzer, zol rinnen iber de bord!

❧

**When you look to the heights,
hold on to your hat.**

Az du kukst oif hoicheh zachen, halt tsu dos hitl.

A wise man knows what he says,
a fool says what he knows.

A kluger vaist vos er zogt, a nar zogt vos er vaist.

꙳

One hand washes the other (and
both wash the face).

Ein hant vasht di tsveiteh

(un beideh vashn dem ponim).

꙳

God takes with one hand, and
gives with the other.

Got nemt mit ain hant un git mit der andereh.

Don't rub your belly when the
little fish is still in the pond.

Patsh zich nit in beicheleh, ven fisheleh zeiner

noch in teicheleh.

⁂

A frequent guest becomes a pest.

A gast oif a vail zeit far a mayll.

A penny at hand is worth a dollar
at a distance.

A noenter groshen iz besser vi a veiter kerbel.

A meowing cat can't catch mice.

A katz vos m'yavket ken kain meiz nit chapen.

❧

**If you can't do as you wish,
do as you can.**

Az me ken nit vi me vil, tut men vi me ken.

❧

**One link snaps and the whole
chain falls apart.**

Brecht zich a ring, tsefalt di gantseh kait.

A half truth is a whole lie.

A halber emes iz amol a ganster ligen.

⚮

**You can't put "thank you" in
your pocket.**

A dank ken men in kesheneh nit legen.

⚮

All that glitters is not gold.

Nit als vos glanst iz gold.

A word is like an arrow—both are
in a hurry to strike.

A vort iz azoi vi a feil—baideh hoben groisseh eil.

⁂

A heavy heart talks a lot.

A shver hartz redt a sach.

⁂

Trying to outsmart everybody is
the greatest folly.

Vellen zein kliger fun alleh iz di gresteh narishkeit.

❧

Man thinks and God laughs.

A mentsh tracht un Got lacht.

A liar must have a good memory.

A ligner darf hoben a guten zickorin.

༆

If you have money, you are wise and
good-looking and can sing well too.

Az me hot gelt, iz men klug un shain un men ken gut zingen.

༆

One old friend is better than two
new ones.

An alter freint iz besser vi nei'eh tsvai.

The food is cooked in a pot and the
plate gets the honor.

Shpeiz kocht men in top un koved krigt der teller.

When a fool goes shopping,
the storekeepers rejoice.

Az a nar gait in mark, fraien zich di kremer.

❧

Money buys everything except
brains.

Far gelt bakumt men alts, nor nit kain saichel.

❧

Words must be weighed and not
counted.

Verter muz men vegen un nit tsailen.

In a quarrel, each side is right.

In toch iz yeder tsad gerecht.

❧

It is easier to be a critic than an author.

Es iz laichter tsu zein a mevaker vi a mechaber.

❧

The pen stings worse than the arrow.

Di pen shist erger vi a fail.

Another man's tidbit smells sweet.

A fremdeh bissen shmekt zis.

❧

A sleepless night is the worst
punishment.

A nacht on shlof iz di gresteh shtrof.

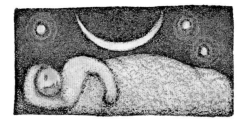

**Suspense is worse than the ordeal
itself.**

Der 'Innu-hadin iz erger vi der din alain.

✂

**Time brings wounds and heals
them.**

Di tseit brengt vunden un hailt vunden.

❧

Love is sweet, but it's nice to have
bread with it.

Di libeh iz zis, mit broit iz zi besser.

**It's good to learn to barber on
someone else's beard.**

Oif a fremder bord iz gut zich tsu lerner sheren.

⤫

The masses are asses.

Der oilem iz a goilem.

⤫

Fools and weeds grow without rain.

Naronim un kropeveh vaksen on regen.

All of life is a struggle.

Dos gantseh leben iz a milchomeh.

❧

If you can't go over, go under.

Az me ken nit ariber, gait men arunter.

❧

Hope for miracles but don't rely on one.

Hof oif nissim noz farloz zich nit oif a nes.

The troubles of a stranger aren't
worth an onion.

A fremdeh tsoreh iz kain tsibeleh ni vert.

It's easier to guard a sack of fleas
than a girl in love.

Es iz laichter tsu hitn a zak flai eider a farlibte maidel.

❧

Easy loves, heavy damages.

Leichteh libes, shvereh shodens.

A man is handsome if he is only
   better looking than the devil.

A man, as er iz shener fun dem teivel, iz er shoin shain.

Dress up a broom and it will also look nice.

Az men batziert a bezem iz er oich shain.

❧

Better caution at first than tears afterwards.

Besser fri'er bevorent aider shpeter bevaint.

❦

The smoothest way is sometimes
full of stones.

Der gleichster veg iz ful mit shtainer.

Ask advice from everyone, but act
with your own mind.

Barat zich mit vemen du vilst;

un tu miten aigenem saichel.

⁂

There is no such thing as a
bad mother.

A shlechteh mameh iz nito.

Little children have big ears.

Kleine kinder hobn groise oiren.

The husband is the boss—if his
wife allows.

Der man iz der balebos—az di veib zaine lozt.

A wicked tongue is worse than an
evil hand.

A baizeh tsung iz erger fun a shlechter hand.

❧

One cross word brings on a quarrel.

Fun a vort vert a kwort.

With honey you can catch more
    flies than with vinegar.

Mit honik ken men chapen mer fligen vi mit essik.

❧

All brides are beautiful; all the
    dead are pious.

Allen kalles zeinen shain; alleh maissim zeinen frum.

❧

Petty thieves are hanged; big
    thieves are pardoned.

Klaineh ganovim hengt men; groisseh shenkt men.

Everything ends in weeping.

Altsding lozt zich ois mit a gevain.

※

**If you eat a bagel, only the hole
remains in your pocket.**

Az men est op dem baigel bleibt in keshene der loch.

※

**You can't chew with someone
else's teeth.**

Men ken nit kaien mit fremde tsein.

Husband and wife are like
one flesh.

Man un veib zeinen ain leib.

Laughter is heard farther
than weeping.

A gelechter hert men veiter vi a gevain.

Once parents used to teach their
children to talk; today children
teach their parents to keep quiet.

Amol flegen di eltern lernen di kinder reden; heint lernen di

kinder di eltern shveigen.

⌘

When the father gives to his son,
both laugh; but when the son gives
to his father, both cry.

Az der tatteh shainkt dem zun, lachen baideh; az der zun

shainkt dem tatten, vainen baideh.

Easy to promise, hard to fulfill.

Gring tsu zogen, shver tsu trogen.

⚘

A wise man hears one word and
understands two.

A kluger farshtait fun ain vort tsvai.

Every ass likes to hear himself
bray.

Yeder aizel hot lib tsu hern vi er alein hirzhet.

He who is aware of his folly is wise.

Der vos farshtait zein narishkeit iz a kluger.

꙾

The gift is not as precious as the
thought.

Es iz nit azoi tei'er der geshank vi der gedank.

꙾

The heaviest burden is an empty
pocket.

Der shversteh ol iz a laidikeh kesheneh.

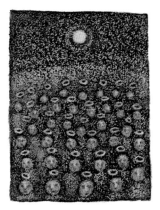

If one could do charity without
money and favors without aggrava-
tion, the world would be
full of saints.

Tsedokeh zol kain gelt nit kosten un g'milas-chassodim kain

agmas-nefesh nit farshafen, volten geven in der velt fil

tsadikim.

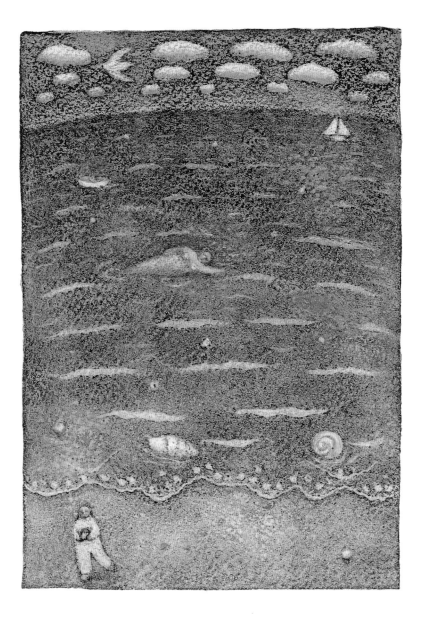

❧

The ocean cannot be emptied with
a spoon.

Me ken dem yam mit a lefell nit ois'shepen.

As the wallet grows, so do the needs.

Ven es vakst der teister, vaksen di baderfenishen.

꒦

Give a pig a finger and he'll want
the whole hand.

Gibb a chazzer a finger vil er de gantseh hand.

꒦

Better to break off an engagement
than a marriage.

Besser di t'no'im tsereissen aider di ketubeh.

Rather alone than with a lowly mate.

Besser gemain, aider alain.

❧

Loans will get you moans.

Borgen macht zorgen.

❧

The door to evil-doing is wide, but
the return gate is narrow.

Arein iz di tir brait, un arois iz zi shmol.

One is greeted according to one's
garb, bidden farewell according to
one's wisdom.

Men bagrist noch di kleider, men bagleit nochen saichel.

❧

Envy breeds hate.

Fun kin'ah vert sin'ah.

That place seems good where
we are not.

Dorten iz gut vu mir seinen nito.

You can't get ahead with keeping
quiet.

Durch shveigen ken men nit shteigen.

&

He who has not tasted the bitter
does not understand the sweet.

Der vos hot nit farzucht bittereh, vaist nit voz zies iz.

&

Better to die upright than to live
on your knees.

Besser tsu shtarben shtai'endik aider tsu leben oif di k'ni.

The world stands on three things:
on money, on money, and on
money.

Oif drei zachen shtait di velt: oif gelt, oif gelt, un oif gelt.

⌘

Don't put off till tomorrow what
you can do today.

Laig nit op oif morgen vos du kenst heint bazorgen.

⌘

He who hesitates is lost.

Vos mer gevart, mer genart.

❧

You can't sit on two horses with one behind.

Mit ein hintn zitst men nit oif tsvei ferd.

**If you stay at home, you won't
wear out your shoes.**

Az men zitst in der haim, tsereist men nit kain shtivel.

Poverty hides wisdom.

Der dales farshtelt di chochma.

⁂

Too much modesty is half conceit.

Tsu fil anives iz a halber shtoltz.

⁂

He who praises himself will be humiliated.

Ver es libt zich alain, shemt zich alain.

When a thief kisses you,
count your teeth.

Ven a ganef kisht darf men zich

di tsein ibertseilen.

When one must, one can.

Az me muz, ken men.

❧

If everybody says so, there's some truth to it.

Az di velt zogt, darf men gloiben.

❧

The most bitter misfortune can be covered up with a smile.

Dem bitersten mazel ken men farshtellen mit a shmaichel.

The smallest vengeance poisons
the soul.

Di klensteh nekomeh farsamt di neshomeh.

⁂

If I would be like someone else,
who will be like me?

Az ich vel zein vi yener, ver vet zein vi ich?

What will become of the sheep if
the wolf is the judge?

Vos ken vern fun di shof az der volf iz der richter?

Still waters run deep.

Shtil vasser grobt tif.

When your enemy falls, don't rejoice,
   but don't pick him up either.

Az der soineh falt, tor men zich nit fraien,

ober men haibt im nit oif.

⚘

If you can't endure the bad,
you'll not live to witness the good.

Az men ken nit iberhalten dos shlechteh,

ken men dos guteh nit derleben.

The reddest apple has a worm in it.

Di roitsteh epel hot a vorm.

Many smiles, few wiles.

Fil shmeichel, veynik saichel.

❧

**If you lie down with the dogs, you
get up with the fleas.**

Az me shloft mit hint shtait men oif mit flai.

❧

**When the stomach is empty,
so is the brain.**

Az der mogen iz laidik iz der moi'ech oich laidik.

Pray that you may never have to
endure all that you can learn to
bear.

Men zol nit gepruft verren tsu vos me ken gevoint verren.

⚭

If your grandmother had a beard,
she'd be your grandfather.

Ven di bobbeh volt gehat a bord, volt zi geven a zaideh.

⚭

If you dig a pit for someone else,
you fall in it yourself.

Az me grubt a grub far yenem, falt men alain arein.

An imaginary illness is worse than
a real one.

An einredenish iz erger vi a krenk.

⚬

Sometimes the remedy is worse
than the disease.

A mol iz der refueh erger fun der makeh.

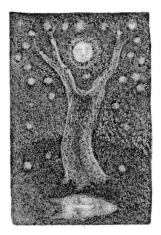

**Heaven and hell can both be had
in this world.**

Ganaiden un gehenem ken men baideh hoben oif der velt.

¢

The heart is small and embraces
the whole wide world.

Di klainer hartz nemt arum di groisseh velt.